La Tierra en acción/Earth in Action

# Fuegos arrasadores/ Wildfires

por/by Matt Doeden

Editora consultora/Consulting Editor: Gail Saunders-Smith, PhD

Consultora/Consultant: Susan L. Cutter, PhD
Distinguida Profesora y Directora de Carolina/Carolina Distinguished Professor and Director
Instituto de Investigación de Peligros y Vulnerabilidad/Hazards & Vulnerability Research Institute
Departamento de Geografía/Department of Geography
University of South Carolina

CAPSTONE PRESS
a capstone imprint

Pebble Plus is published by Capstone Press,
151 Good Counsel Drive, P.O. Box 669, Mankato, Minnesota 56002.
www.capstonepub.com

 Books published by Capstone Press are manufactured with paper containing at least 10 percent post-consumer waste.

*Library of Congress Cataloging-in-Publication Data*
Doeden, Matt.
  [Wildfires. Spanish & English]
  Fuegos arrasadores = Wildfires / by Matt Doeden.
    p. cm.—(Pebble Plus bilingüe. La tierra en acción = Pebble Plus bilingual. Earth in action)
  Includes index.
  Summary: "Describes wildfires, how they occur, and the ways people can stay safe--in both English and Spanish"—Provided by publisher.
  Text in English and Spanish.
  ISBN 978-1-4296-6120-1 (library binding)
  1. Wildfires—Juvenile literature. I. Title. II. Title: Wildfires. III. Series.
SD421.23.D6418 2011
363.37'9—dc22                                                        2010040926

**Editorial Credits**
Erika L. Shores, editor; Strictly Spanish, translation services; Heidi Thompson, designer;
    Danielle Ceminsky, bilingual book designer; Laura Manthe, production specialist

**Photo Credits**
FEMA News Photo/Andrea Booher, 1, 19
Getty Images Inc./David McNew, 21; The Image Bank/Jose Luis Pelaez, 15; Justin Sullivan, 13; Milos Bicanski, 17;
    Photographer's Choice/Kathy Quirk-Syvertsen, 9; Stone/Bryce Duffy, 11
iStockphoto/David Parsons, cover
Shutterstock/Denis and Yulia Pogostins, 7; Peter Weber, 5

## Note to Parents and Teachers

The La Tierra en acción/Earth in Action set supports national science standards related to earth science. This book describes and illustrates wildfires in both English and Spanish. The images support early readers in understanding the text. The repetition of words and phrases helps early readers learn new words. This book also introduces early readers to subject-specific vocabulary words, which are defined in the Glossary section. Early readers may need assistance to read some words and to use the Table of Contents, Glossary, Internet Sites, and Index sections of the book.

Printed in the United States of America in North Mankato, Minnesota.
092010    005933CGS11

# Table of Contents

# Tabla de contenidos

# What Is a Wildfire?

A wildfire is an outdoor fire that burns out of control. Wildfires burn grass, trees, homes, and everything else in their paths.

# ¿Qué es un fuego arrasador?

Un fuego arrasador es un incendio al aire libre que arde fuera de control. Los fuegos arrasadores queman pasto, árboles, casas y todo lo que encuentran a su paso.

Most wildfires happen when
grass, trees, and soil are dry.
Wildfires usually happen
in summer and fall.

---

La mayoría de los fuegos arrasadores
ocurre cuando el pasto, los árboles
y el suelo están secos. Los fuegos
arrasadores normalmente ocurren
en el verano y el otoño.

# What Causes Wildfires?

People cause most wildfires. Some fires start when a campfire is left alone to burn out. Other times people start fires on purpose.

# ¿Cuáles son las causas de los fuegos arrasadores?

Las personas causan la mayoría de los fuegos arrasadores. Algunos incendios empiezan cuando una fogata se deja sin supervisión para que se consuma. En otras ocasiones las personas inician los incendios a propósito.

Lightning can start fires. Lightning may strike dry trees or plants. Strong winds make wildfires spread quickly.

---

Los rayos pueden causar incendios. Los rayos pueden caer sobre plantas o árboles secos. Los vientos fuertes hacen que los fuegos arrasadores se extiendan rápidamente.

# Wildfire Safety

Wildfires are dangerous. People should leave the area if a fire is near their home. Leaving is called evacuating.

# La seguridad y los fuegos arrasadores

Los fuegos arrasadores son peligrosos. Las personas deben abandonar el área si hay un incendio cerca de su casa. A esto se lo llama evacuar.

Sometimes people cannot
get away in time. At home,
they should stay away from
outside walls and windows.

———————————————————

En ocasiones, las personas no
pueden irse a tiempo. En casa,
deben mantenerse alejados de las
paredes exteriores y las ventanas.

People outside need to avoid heat and smoke. They should cover their mouth and nose. They should find a place with few plants and lay down.

---

Las personas que están afuera deben evitar el calor y el humo. Deben taparse la boca y la nariz. Deben encontrar un lugar que tenga pocas plantas y recostarse.

# Fighting Wildfires

Firefighters try to stop wildfires.

They use axes to clear plants

so the fire cannot spread.

# Al combate de los fuegos arrasadores

Los bomberos tratan de detener

los fuegos arrasadores. Usan hachas

para despejar las plantas para que

el incendio no pueda extenderse.

Firefighters pour water and chemicals on wildfires. Firefighters work to keep people and their homes safe.

---

Los bomberos rocían los fuegos arrasadores con agua y sustancias químicas. Los bomberos trabajan para mantener la seguridad de las personas y sus casas.

# Glossary

**chemical**—a substance made for a specific purpose

**evacuate**—to get away from danger by leaving an area

**firefighter**—a person who is trained to put out fires or stop them from spreading

**lightning**—a strong burst of electricity that passes between a cloud and the ground

# Internet Sites

FactHound offers a safe, fun way to find Internet sites related to this book. All of the sites on FactHound have been researched by our staff.

Here's all you do:

Visit www.facthound.com

Type in this code: 9781429661201

Check out projects, games and lots more at
www.capstonekids.com

# Glosario

**el bombero**—una persona capacitada para extinguir incendios o evitar que se extiendan

**evacuar**—alejarse del peligro abandonando un área

**el rayo**—una descarga fuerte de electricidad que pasa entre una nube y la tierra

**la sustancia química**—una sustancia hecha para un fin específico

# Sitios de Internet

FactHound brinda una forma segura y divertida de encontrar sitios de Internet relacionados con este libro. Todos los sitios en FactHound han sido investigados por nuestro personal.

Esto es todo lo que tienes que hacer:

Visita www.facthound.com

Ingresa este código: 9781429661201

# Index

# Índice